J
629.22
Bar
Barrett
Trucks

R336886
9.40

PICTURE LIBRARY

TRUCKS

PICTURE LIBRARY
TRUCKS

N. S. Barrett

Franklin Watts

London   New York   Sydney   Toronto

© 1984 Franklin Watts Ltd

First published in Great Britain
    1984 by
Franklin Watts Ltd
12a Golden Square
London W1

First published in the USA by
Franklin Watts Inc
387 Park Avenue South
New York
N.Y. 10016

First published in Australia by
Franklin Watts
1 Campbell Street
Artarmon, NSW 2064

UK ISBN: 0 86313 193 X
US ISBN: 0-531-03723-1
Library of Congress Catalog Card
Number: 84-50700

Printed in Italy

Designed by
McNab Design

Photographs by
Australian News and Information Service
British Leyland
ERF
Foden
Ford Motor Company
Scania
Shell Photo Service
Volvo
ZEFA

Illustrated by
Tony Bryan

Technical Consultant
John Parsons

Contents

Introduction

Trucks are the largest vehicles on the road. They deliver most of the materials we need. Some trucks deliver freight from factories to warehouses. Other trucks then take the freight to shops. Special trucks are used to deliver gasoline to gas stations. Some trucks have one or more trailers for carrying extra loads.

△ A dump truck is loaded with coal. When it unloads, the body tips up and the load slides out.

Trucks are also used to deliver furniture to people's homes. Some trucks have cranes specially fitted for lifting heavy loads. Other trucks can tip up to make it easy to dump their loads.

There are many other kinds of trucks that have special uses, such as collecting garbage or fighting fires.

△ A fleet of trucks, neatly parked, is ready for work on building sites.

The truck

The tractor unit of a
combination truck

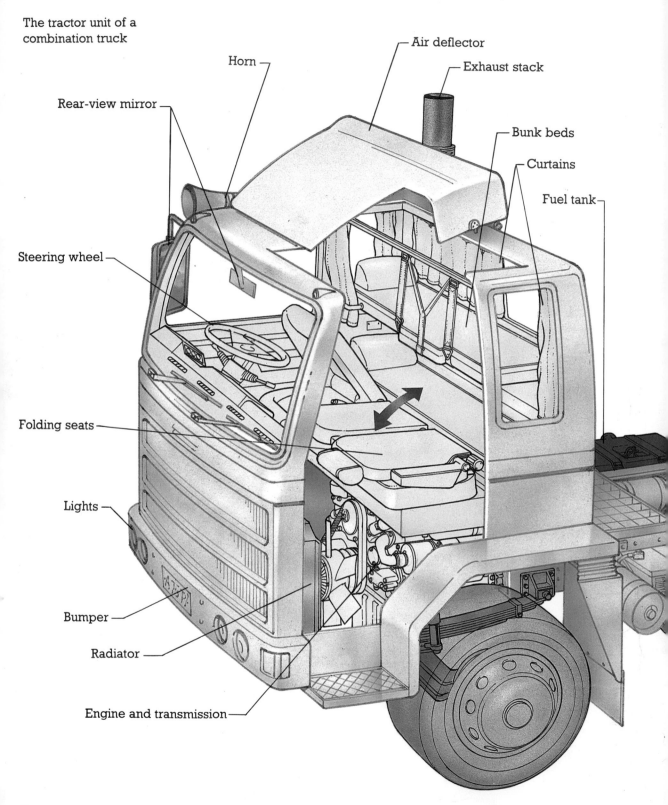

Horn

Air deflector

Exhaust stack

Rear-view mirror

Bunk beds

Curtains

Fuel tank

Steering wheel

Folding seats

Lights

Bumper

Radiator

Engine and transmission

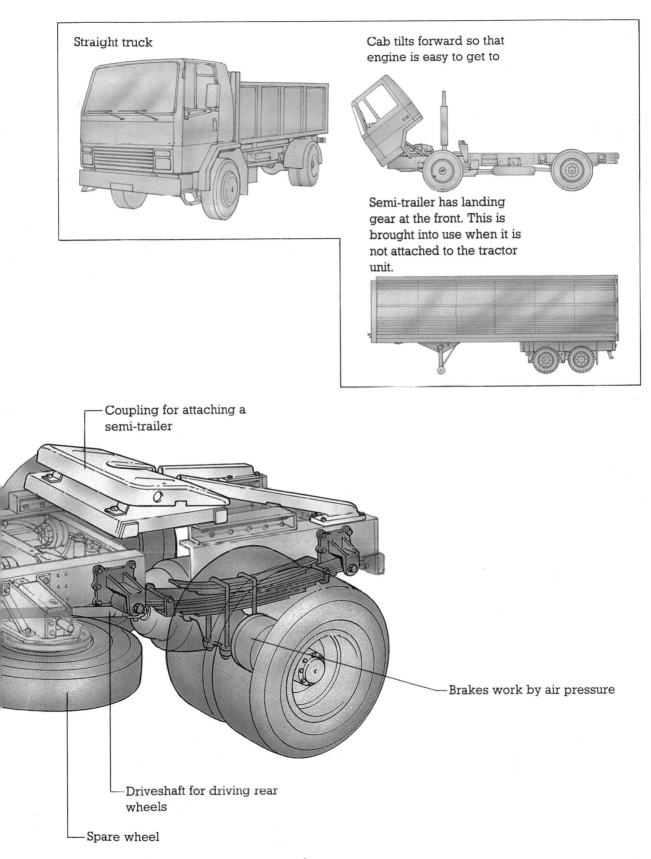

Straight truck

Cab tilts forward so that engine is easy to get to

Semi-trailer has landing gear at the front. This is brought into use when it is not attached to the tractor unit.

Coupling for attaching a semi-trailer

Brakes work by air pressure

Driveshaft for driving rear wheels

Spare wheel

Uses of trucks

Trucks must have powerful engines to carry heavy loads. Some trucks have as many as 20 wheels to support the weight of their loads.

Trucks that have the cab, engine and freight-carrying part in one piece are called straight trucks. Trucks that are made in two parts are called combination trucks. They have a tractor and a semi-trailer.

△ Auto haulers have specially designed platforms for carrying car bodies. The upper platform swings back and down for easy unloading.

10

△A dump truck begins to empty its load. The driver can raise the body of the truck by using the controls in his cab.

◁A tank truck delivers fuel to a working site. Tankers carry liquids. They must have strong bodies.

11

Trucks are used in places that other forms of transport cannot reach. Material going by rail, sea, or air is usually delivered by trucks to stations, docks, and airports. At the other end, trucks collect the materials and take them on the last part of their journey by road. Trucks are also used to carry materials over long distances.

△Some trucks used for carrying logs have their own cranes. The driver can load the logs onto the truck himself.

△ A truck with an extra trailer can carry a lot of hay. An open load like this has to be carefully secured with ropes.

◁ The body of this truck has a separate opening for each barrel. This makes loading and unloading easier.

13

△A truck and trailer carrying thousands of racing pigeons. The pigeons are all let out together and fly back to their homes.

◁A special transporter built to carry a motor racing team and their cars and equipment.

△Refrigerator trucks are used for carrying food. They keep the food at the correct temperature so that it does not spoil on the journey.

◁Special trucks are used for servicing street lights. The driver can lift and lower himself with controls in the servicing platform.

Off-highway trucks

Some trucks are built for use off the roads. They are called off-highway trucks or off-road trucks. They work on rough ground and uneven tracks, often in very muddy conditions. Some are used on building sites to carry materials and heavy machinery. Many off-highway trucks have cranes so that the driver can load and unload them himself.

▽ Big dump trucks are used for shifting earth. They carry heavy loads over rough ground, and unload it by tipping. They have huge tires, often as big as their cabs.

△ This airfield truck is like a road recovery vehicle. It is used when small aircraft break down or crash.

◁ Off-road trucks that travel fast over rough ground have their bodies set high so that they are not damaged by rocks.

Off-highway trucks are used in mines and quarries. Trucks that carry heavy machinery have low beds to make loading easier.

Powerful engines are needed for carrying heavy loads up steep slopes. Special tires are used for driving over rough or muddy surfaces. Off-highway trucks must be tough to stand up to jolts.

△ This truck is called a low-bed. It has a trailer with a low body to make it easier to load very heavy machinery.

△This truck has its own crane and "clamshell" for loading earth.

◁Desert trucks are carefully sealed to keep out the sand and dust. They have special tires that do not sink into the sand. Their engine drives four or even six wheels. This helps to get them moving if they become stuck.

19

Highway heroes

Big trucks are much larger than other vehicles on the highways. Truck drivers spend most of their time on the road. Because of their courtesy and helpfulness to other drivers, they are called heroes of the road.

In many places, truckers talk to each other on their "CB" radio. They use a language of their own.

▽ This truck has six wheels on the tractor and another sixteen on its semi-trailer for hauling this very heavy load of steel. The cargo is kept in place by chains, but the truck must be driven slowly, especially around corners.

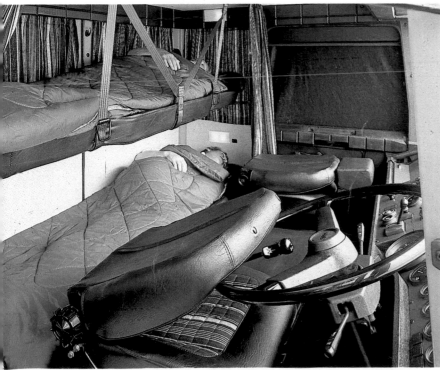

△ A truck leaves the docks with its cargo. Trucks pick up cargo after it has been unloaded from a ship. Sometimes, trucks are carried from port to port by a ship.

◁ The inside of the cab of a long-distance truck. The seats fold forward when the sleeping compartment is being used.

Long-distance truckers sometimes haul their loads over thousands of miles. In some parts of the world, they may drive for several hours before coming to a town.

Many trucks have sleeping compartments. In parts of Australia, Canada, and the USA, tractor units pull as many as three trailers. These are called road trains or triples.

△ A road train carrying gasoline in the desert region of northern Australia. Trucks like these would be too big for use on busy roads. But they are just right for areas with few towns and little traffic.

▷ A truck picks up its cargo from a container terminal. Container trucks have flat cargo areas for carrying these standard-sized boxes.

22

▷Trucks may have to work in dusty places and carry dirty loads, but many truckers keep them in perfect, shining condition.

Fire engines

Fire engines have to carry a lot of special equipment. They have water tanks, hoses and pumps to shoot the water out in a strong jet. Some fire trucks carry ladders that can be raised by powerful motors. They have to reach as high as 100 ft (30 m) or more. Airport fire trucks, or crash trucks, have to move very quickly over short distances.

△ Airfield fire trucks carry a special liquid that comes out as powerful jets of foam.

△Stabilizing legs keep the fire truck steady when the ladders are in use.

◁The water jets on this fire truck can be directed from the ground. They are controlled electrically.

The story of trucks

The first trucks

The first trucks were small. They were really motor cars with a few changes in the body. They had the same engines as motor cars, which meant that they could carry only small loads. But they were faster than horse-drawn vehicles, and soon became popular. About 80 years ago, large trucks were driven by steam engines.

△ Wooden panels were used to enclose trucks.

△ A simple truck of nearly 60 years ago.

More horsepower

The first motorized trucks were expensive and they often broke down. Horses were cheaper and more reliable. But as better and more powerful engines were produced, trucks began to replace horses. The size of engines was measured in a unit called horsepower. A 20 hp (horsepower) engine had the same pulling power as 20 horses.

Protecting the cargo

The first trucks carried their cargo on an open flat bed or in an open box. Trucks like these are still used today, because they are easy to load and unload. But for keeping cargo safe and protecting it from the weather, the bodywork must be built up and enclosed. Wooden panels were used for making the bodies of trucks and vans. Now they are made from metals such as steel or aluminum.

△ A modern combination truck.

28

Combinations

Combination trucks were produced in the late 1930s. The first ones were unsteady, especially when going around corners. The coupling, which connects the tractor with the semi-trailer, was gradually improved, and is now called the "fifth wheel." But it was another twenty years before combinations were really safe. Now they are very popular.

Dump trucks

The first vehicles for carrying loose materials, such as sand or

△ An early dump truck.

coal, were flat-bedded trucks with sides that could be taken off or let down on hinges. Workers used shovels to load and unload them. It was not long before someone thought of tilting the body so that the contents could

be tipped out. The first ones had long screws at the front which had to be wound up by hand. Now, powerful "rams" are used. These are worked by liquid pressure and are controlled from inside the cab.

Over the engine

Most early trucks had their engines under hoods, just like cars. The first trucks to have the driver's cab over the engine were built in the early 1930s. This allows more load space behind. It also gives the driver a better view of the road ahead.

Trailers

One way to increase the space for cargo is to attach trailers. A trailer may be attached to another trailer, or behind a straight truck, by use of a "dolly." Trucks may have two, three or more trailers.

△ A truck with a draw-bar trailer.

Facts and records

Big tires

Large dump trucks have huge tires. The tires on some trucks are 12 ft (3.65 m) across. They stand twice as high as a tall person. Each tire costs more than a new car.

△ An off-highway dump truck.

Racing trucks

Some motor sports have races for trucks. In drag racing, two vehicles called dragsters race over a short straight track. Trucks used in drag racing have special engines. The races last only a few seconds. Trucks also take part in long-distance races, such as the desert races held in parts of Africa, the United States and Mexico.

△ A customized truck from Thailand.

Custom trucks

Some drivers like to decorate their trucks. They paint them in bright colors. They also make other changes in the look of the truck. Vehicles changed in this way are sometimes called custom trucks.

△ An Australian dragster.

Glossary

Air deflector
A panel on top of the cab of some trucks. It deflects air up and over the trailer. In this way, it cuts down the slowing effect of the air.

Cab
The driver's compartment.

Combination truck
A combination truck has a tractor and a semi-trailer. The semi-trailer may be taken off and another one put in its place.

Container truck
A flat-bedded truck used for carrying a container, a large, standard-sized box that holds the cargo.

Coupling (fifth wheel)
The coupling connects the trailer to a tractor unit. Two trailers are coupled by a "dolly".

Low-bed
A type of truck used for carrying heavy machinery. It has a trailer with a carrying platform close to the ground.

Off-highway truck
A truck built for use off the roads. Many types of off-highway truck are not allowed to use the roads. They might have to be taken to a work site in parts.

Semi-trailer
A trailer that is coupled to a tractor unit. It has no wheels in front. It sits on the back of the tractor.

Straight truck
A truck that has its load area, motor and cab in one unt.

Tanker
A truck used for carrying liquids, such as gasoline or milk.

Tractor
The power unit, or cab, of a combination truck.

Trailer
The part of a truck that is towed. It carries cargo. Trailers can have any number of wheels, depending on the use they are intended for. Semi-trailers do not have wheels at the front.

Van
An enclosed truck, with the driver's cabin and cargo area built as one piece under the same roof. Enclosed trailers are also called vans.

31

Index